KW-339-815

THE MIDDLEMAN

David Cavanagh

POETRY LIBRARY
SOUTH BANK CENTRE
ROYAL FESTIVAL HALL
LONDON
SE1 8XX

salmonpoetry

Published in 2003 by
Salmon Publishing Ltd.,
Cliffs of Moher, County Clare, Ireland
Website: www.salmonpoetry.com
email: info@salmonpoetry.com

Copyright © David Cavanagh, 2003

ISBN 1 903392 31 4

All rights reserved. No part of this publication may be reproduced or transmitted in any form or by any means, electronic or mechanical, including photography, recording, or any information storage or retrieval system, without permission in writing from the publisher. The book is sold subject to the condition that it shall not, by way of trade or otherwise, be lent, resold or otherwise circulated without the publisher's prior consent in any form of binding or cover other than that in which it is published and without a similar condition, including this condition, being imposed on the subsequent purchaser.

Cover photo of Karl Wallenda from the Circus World Museum, Baraboo, WI
Cover design & typesetting by Siobhán Hutson

Poetry Library
095229
COPY NO. 2
Royal Festival Hall
on the South Bank
sbc
Poetry Library
Royal Festival Hall, Level 5
London SE1 8XX
Telephone 020 7921 0943
Books may be renewed by telephone
Date due back
WITHDRAWN FROM THE POETRY LIBRARY

To the memory of my parents,
Agnes Mary Cavanagh and David Peter Cavanagh

Acknowledgments

Grateful acknowledgment goes to the editors of the following publications in which some of these poems have appeared:

The Antigonish Review, Avenue, The Burlington Review, The Fiddlehead Review, Gihon River Review, Green Mountains Review, The Malahat Review, Poetry Ireland Review, the chapbook *Ethic = Visceral* from Wood Thrush Books, and *Breaking the Blame Chain* from Kendall/Hunt Publishing.

My deep thanks go to the family members, friends, and other poets who have assisted me with insights about the poems and have given crucial encouragement. In particular, I want to thank Sharon Webster, Greg Delanty, and Aaron Thomas.

Contents

Call It

Call it some fashionable moniker
if you like, call it a mid-life thing,
a passage, a phase, a burr in the saddle,
call it something dismissive, mildly
self-mocking, a zit of the soul,
a speed bump on life's interstate,
or get classical, call it a Dante thing,
a ring of hell, a *mezzo del cammin* thing,
call it whatever you damn well want,
tell yourself you'll get over it,
call it something half-way attractive,
your long-awaited break for freedom,
breakout, breakaway, or better yet,
tinge it with irony (very Gucci!),
call it breakdown, breakup, way way up.
Or if you can get past the LLBeanness
of it all, the Oprah and Regis of it,
if you can get past the self-help book
(I'm a Shithead, You're a Shithead),
call it not wanting ever to die.

Call it jealous – those deep damned gods,
those immortal deadbeat dads, those
eternal diaphanous moms, call it
wanting to taste the true deep drop
before you give over; call it
looking around, looking behind,
looking ahead, seeing only dregs, the tip,
the bit, the mainstreet stim and tease,
the artificial bottled extract of what
you had planned, what you had hoped,
what you thought you would surely
do. Call it bewildered, befuddled,

THE POETRY LIBRARY

beleaguered, call it wanting more than ever
seems available. Call it a house half built,
a blueprint lost in a drawer you dread
opening, that pile of forgotten plans;
call it utterly pissed off, at youth, for example,
no, not at youth, poor saps, youthfulness;
the lithe, sexy swagger of it; call it sickly
green; call it stiff in the morning but
in all the wrong places; call it getting up,
call it numb, call it crazy blind in pain
of numbness, call it putting on the shirt,
the tie, the socks, the shoes, top to bottom,
out the door, all armoured up, call it
the quiet roar, and more, call it
what it is, for once, just call it
what it is, and c'mon, get over it,
call it your life.

Dawn

again, like a ghost in a movie
comes, the softest of fade-ins. Brooding
cedars, dark cathedral columns. Contour,
colour, forming and re-forming, shaggy,
drooping gods on the back-lit, backyard set.

The soul in training, grey bird taking air.
Not flight, but breath, the fledgling
awkward gulps. At 50, at daybreak,
that new, that unscripted, that tremulous, swallowing

As If

As if playing one of those 50 cent
    try-your-road-skill machines –
slip 4 bits to eternity and watch
    the road come at you.

Steer, baby, steer.
    A curve, a wreckage
to veer around, the road
        at you faster
    all the time
while time recedes. Memory
    is what you cannot afford

to be without. The yellow lilies
    Sharon brought for the table
yesterday are central,
        not to forget the yellow placemats
    placed there a week or maybe
more ago.

A journalist asks if poetry is
    political. Trick question. Answer:
emphatically, NO. YES.
How do you define faith?
        I use words.

As if inside a humid car
rain pelting the glass and roof
    in gusts to get at you
who would like, simply,
    to open the car door and be drenched.

More road.
    How close is a car
to caring?

As if windshield were not also brittle
clear silicon lens surrounding.
        Which end of the camera
are you at this evening?

An old woman hides money in a cup
in a cupboard, in several cups and cupboards
because of the thieves, she says, who visit
her kitchen.

    "You belong to me," she levels
at her children, tucks them away
    inside that perfectly safe mug.

More road.

    As if travelling in your car
were a kind of therapeutic dream
        on the road
        cover ground
        make good time
        keep your distance.
As if keeping your distance
were a way of keeping your hair
    unmussed, or at all.

    "Let me buy you a drink,"
the one you are serving me
    with just the right amount of
politeness, humour, disdain.

Waitress in blue,
a stunning silver bangle on a strong
tanned wrist, and so much barely
contained.

Measure how far you've gone and how
skillfully. An ambulance out of nowhere.
A budding alder and a momentary
lapse into feeling authentic.

A blank page asks for commitment.

Across the way, two share an intimate
salad, but he makes a slow-motion
stab for the last wedge
of tomato.

"Objects in mirror
are closer than they appear."

As if driving into a mirror,
you are so used to seeing yourself
reversed from left to right.

Think about the geography
of brake pedals and accelerators
and what you have been pushing
all these years.

Moods of It

it was rich   it was the moon   it was strange
like a pearl being turned in some old Thelma's
hand   it was breathing the deep sharp air
of risk   it was the high note left hanging
by the trumpeter with white shoes in the lakeside bar
it was the lake skating away from the broken-down pier
it was morning   it was what we offered
it was the slim glance you passed me
it was your legs round me gentle   the trust
that trees have   standing like questions
it was leafy   it was something
we have no longer a name for

Montreal Blues

I come from disappointed people.
Mowers of late autumn lawns,

pushed-mowed and cross-cut into squares,
the cut grass caught in a canvas hook-on

emptied over and over into battered trash cans.
I come from ironers of underwear,

a people who stretched wool socks by the dozen
on wooden frames hung from basement pipes,

a father who spent forty-two years
hating a job to feed us, which he did;

his first job tearing used carbons all night
1934 long to reinsert into blank order pads

for use by busy sellers all the bright next day;
his last job filling blank order pads 1976

with thousand-dollar sales and taking crap
because he couldn't learn French in a city

full of chic he could no longer understand,
though he was proud of this Montroyal,

showed visitors its sights and history
like a parent holding out photos of a child

who somehow has outgrown and now ignores him.

Buzz

In the gone tomorrow
world of bread labour,
this here today, this 40-hour
hour, this mucked mind
of paperwork, I sit
upright, my rubber soles
flat on the floor,
my hands shifting
this that there,
a worker bee dazed
with momentum
and the nectar of approval,
stuck hard on honey lust,
fairly buzzed with it,
buying it, bought.

The Drone

Born strangely from unfertilized egg,
with no stinger and only one job,
to mate with ye old queen bee, this idler
lollygags, fed by the sterile women of the house,
until he gets his shot, which probably
never comes, considering he is one of hundreds
and her majesty chooses only half a dozen
to get it on with and bring forth the royal brood.
So one must assume his lounging is filled with
anxiety – all dressed up for the party
of a lifetime, then bounced at the door
by a bunch of worker women. Come fall,
he is bounced again, this time right out
of the colony, left on his own, untutored
in meal preparation, sans stinger,
with no choice, in the end, but to starve or freeze.
His story, the tale of the drone, metaphorical
as it may or may not be, is perhaps
the origin of the phrase: "poor dumb fucker."

The Way to Work

A scarf of fog, soft and heavy, slung
along a ridge of autumn hills, evergreens
dark between grey and sky. A car
speeding into the scene, blue-coated worker
behind the wheel, still except for small
steering motions of arms and hands;
thinking sporadically of meetings, reports,
dealings ahead, admiring the splash of day
against a red-orange tree, squinting into the dazzle
of last night's frost yielding on a sun-soaked field.

He lifts his chin, stretches his neck
against the knot of tie. Something is missing,
he thinks, these days. His sense of self,
and the sensation of self forgotten –
that handblown, speckled space where time
collapses, or else expands, hesitancy
vanishes, and you move unhurried
in sureness, grace – then the slow, strange
seconds of coming to, as from a dream,
or like the tingling when a numbed hand
or foot wakes up, blood finding its baffled way
back into limb. And you are normal again
at your table, or by a lake; you notice
yourself noticing the fire of sky
cooling in the waters of the evening.

These things, he tells himself, are missing.
Rolls the car window halfway down. A rush
of shocking air, a cold he would like to taste,
a trolling tongue of mist, he imagines,
slipping in from the hills across his throat.

Dear English Teacher

1

your course outline says i will become
        proficient with words

well i've been here all semester
        where are they?

2

the truth is
i don't wanna talk
like you

so you can go
fuck yourself

and you know what i mean

3

you tell me there are words
    i don't know you
            your language
my language
only is this tearing stretch of my
events against the telling

when i am older i will kill you
word-hoarder
    (your throat – my knife
    your tongue – my reddened stick)
who knew and did not share

in this skull i live alone
wonder how the others
    grope their ways
how the letters fit together into hate
how long the jellied brain must sag
        against its silence

when i move and reach with language
    (and i will
    i will fashion cryptic jagged graphics
    make words out of brain tissue
    carve them into smiles)
            you will crumple
you will be the crushed sentence i have stuttered out
these years

you will be the sounded rage i cannot have
or find

to love you with

The Ocean I Would Move In

Waves of you
wash me softly
your currents turn me
deeps enfold me
woman even your plant
life holds me
I love its green
dance its sway
of greeting
when you smile at me
I am carried near
shimmers of reefs
of ancient colour

I warn you
I am not used
to your underwater world
I am surface creature
metallic in sun
but these days I admit
there is a flowing
smooth dark glide
that never seems to want
for air

I even begin to like the feel
of these gills you gave me
laughing

How a Weekend Goes

joni singing of coyotes and a prisoner of the freeway;
it must be nearly midnight here; i am many places;
what do exhaustion and getting drunk have to do with
...that woman's thighs, for example, ample
enough to drift me to the next park bench where
someone is intent on reading news of boredom;
people, it seems, are selling shares in everything;
at the end of the lake, the jumping of fish remains
a sound you cannot see; on the joni mitchell record
the trumpet is slithery, i want to reach you but
the vision does not bend to this unsightly grammar;
the woman in the restaurant with the jaunty breasts
wants to tell me all about question marks, but first
i have to mention the relish jars that sharon
is boiling while joni is singing of icarus again; they are
leaning like dapper old men in the stew-pot while bubbles
escape from underneath. this is the most fun i have
had in months; i may have to be sleepless, even;
something tells me the sunflower in the front yard doesn't
give a damn if i am drunk; i admire that; it is a silly
bent-over showerhead of a thing, and why not; pat metheny's
guitar lick is a silver limousine on a downtown street just
after a rain has left the roadway shiny and black and humourous;
you by the bar, can you take another sip for me, then cross your
legs, then laugh; that would be a generous combination; i want
someone to discourse on the politics of semicolons, but not for
long; last night the trees were shaggy applause for the cool blazing
notes of the stars; i was looking straight up through branches, and i
felt tiny, i felt like the only one seeing that particular angle
of pine boughing black into a burst of galaxy; days
earlier, in the hospital, a woman in a wheelchair did
not get on my elevator when it stopped at her floor;
she waved with a very intelligent gaze and wheeled herself away;

THE POETRY LIBRARY

doors closed and i ascended; by the time i got off i was nowhere
again; i want to tell you about sex with a beautiful woman
but i don't know how; later, the canoe took us to where
trees were ancient as herons, lily pads relaxed around us,
the canoe sliding over them, a thing of aluminum and rivets
almost as beautiful for its going as the water it slipped through,
arms moving it as it seemed to want, shoulder sockets,
triceps, hands connected through wooden paddles to
lake where the lilies laughed up from split green circles;
i could tell you perhaps about the way her arm curved
back above her head, but maybe you get the picture; it seems
quiet now, and you should know that the herons *were* there,
a pair of them, probably with a nest in the weeds, and we
were watching; i can't begin to describe where her hip
turned into thigh, and we felt small and graced;

Goldfish Talk #1

In a black pond buttressed
with ton blocks of marble
upended like a buckled ancient theatre –
        goldfish
the size of shimmering evening gloves.

In a living room's bowl
they have shrunk to
dangled earrings. Such brilliant

calm astonishes, such perfect
adaptation; and me so
out of place at parties.

Goldfish Talk #2

Since buying the goldfish I find myself
more interested in swimming,

less talkative, more inclined to undulation,
the quick flick out of harm's way.

Notice glass houses everywhere. I'm
fish-eyed with wondering who is looking in.

Ah, but the swimming, the grace,
the wordless way through wet that yields,

surrounds, and makes of movement
a memory sinuously turning and returning.

I am slowly busy remembering myself.
My drowned teenage years, for instance,

the hot lonely need of them, survive now
in halting cliché, opaque as a cracked 45.

I decide to go down for a look.
At the Y swim dozens of slow laps,

legs scissoring the surface, goggled
face-down eyes scanning the painted

bottom for a healthy pair of lungs.
Nothing but black lines and aqua spaces

quavering under and away from my regular
language of manic bubbles.

Goldfish Talk #3

Beyond mere goldfish grace
which I admire, which I hunger
too deeply for, which pulls me
like a broken weed some days
after it, fishtailing, sodden;

what I understand
some days beyond all hunger
and grace is the ruined

wall of ancestry
rearing in their still cold
porthole eyes.

It's So Much Like Missiles

One day you hear they've been fired –
the missiles I mean – you imagine them
curving like so many Golden Gates
between a hundred cities, serene vapour trails
with some message you cannot imagine,
and don't have to, for you know
you have one half of one hour.

And everything's suddenly simple,
like the time you heard your father had died,
long-distance the phone clicking
softly as a heart while you felt everything
freeze in your tiny kitchen, altered,
and impossibly unchanged.

And the funny thing is not that they've gone
up – the missiles I mean – but that they remind
you of something you didn't do, some words
you didn't say, just didn't take the trouble
to say, like the time you were leaving town,
and a friend, and you never told her how much
she meant to you, and you never saw her again.

Now missiles are flying, and it's just
like when your father died, and the visit
you'd put off became a dream-train you lived
on nightly, dark train pounding on smoothest
rails of guilt, and never ever arriving.

The thing about what's unsaid is
you can never take it back.
If you had made that final visit
you'd have fought with him, most probably,

over Trudeau, or disarmament, something
not too close. And it would have been
furious and futile till it hit you
that this time he was dying,
and you'd have stopped, and so would he,
both of you sheepish, feeling
each other sheepish, awkwardness
your last strange sharing.

But the thing about not visiting, not
loving enough to say or fight or apologize
or see something new between you –
the thing about not saying is

it's so much like those missiles
up there, on the way, on the final way,
so undone, so unsaid, and so impossible
to take back.

Last Visit

Slow as March's receding snow
he moved along the hospital wall,

talked calmly of his funeral,
waved away our foolish talk

about not giving up; could not afford
the lie we wanted for each other;

looked away when we talked like that,
as if listening to some hardened

inner voice leading him now,
some ancient deity returned to take

him back; the cancer hot and leaping
in him, cells darkening like lava;

his body a disaster, a momentum
he was forced to live within, a flood,

a flash-fire, as in the solid wooden sheds
he loved to build near pines on mountain

land he'd found some 16 years ago
and used to carve some sense out of the life

he slogged through in the routine dust
of Montreal. Where now he waited to die.

It had happened to us before, his brother
swollen with death before his time,

and the strength he'd given everyone
out of disease. "Take it easy, just

take it easy," he'd told me at the last,
and it was not the words but the tone

that made the gift important, as if
he'd seen something, finally,

perfectly true and simple. And now
my father helping us accept this strange

cliff-face of his dying, even as he tried
to know the depths and clefts of it himself,

me wondering later why this family
needs the precipice of losing life

before it can love well.
Conversation floated in the room

unreal as TV, until he moved away
to sit on the edge of the bed,

his back to us as he buzzed the nurse
for morphine – and him so polite

only pain like a crazed fist
could make him turn from visitors.

For ten minutes he faced the intercom
as if praying, though he had never believed

anything beyond what he could see.
Now he waited for an answer, a pill

to smother the shriek his body had become,
his back bent away from us, old, brittle.

He reached for a water glass
and knocked it off the table.

From across the room, helpless,
I watched it on its sure, weightless

way to floor – the shatter of a shape,
shards everywhere, so random,

or else in patterns I could not
seem to understand.

Stringing Lights

for Dave, Sr.

So mild for December that I rouse from a cloudy
Sunday torpor to string the Christmas lights.
As he did, year after year, on the fir tree and balcony
till the tree grew higher than he could have imagined,
but still he went with it, buying more lights, hauling
out taller stepladders, then the aluminum extension type,
nearly as high as the house or so it seemed to me, the reds,
greens, yellows, blues, winding the boughs in brightness.

But before that, the mess of wires and bulbs tangling up
the kitchen like bewildered snakes with multi-coloured eyes
waiting for some spark. Which he provided. Fedora,
parka, and up the precarious ladder on chilling afternoons
that always ran into evening with him out there alone,
we kids, bored and bone-cold with standing, having left him
for living room, munchies, TV; him out there leaning way right
to place a red one on that outlaw branch on the side away
from the wrought-iron rail; mother inside fretting
over dinner and downfall while he stretched and stretched
and finally, long after the meal had gone grim with warming,
came in flushed with cold and victory and maybe something more.

So now I run strands of tiny modern bulbs up the latticework
and around the wooden balcony on a house a hundred miles away.
Thinking as much of him as of the job. I wonder if he looked
forward to this time of stringing lights or if it just overtook him,
as it does me, a sudden swell that breaks up concentration
on the mysterious failure of days; something to do, why not, then
the surprise of interest spreading like the burn on cheeks just in
from cold, desire to see these lights run round the house just
as one envisions, nails to hold up wires, twist-ties to clamp

them down. Then – after all the climbing, stringing,
blowing on fingers – the instant of plugging in, and the scene
irrepressibly bright! Despite everything, deep uncollared
delight, the bite of memory, on the short, laden days of the year.

For Agnes Mary

Rain in my 42nd year, soft as forgiveness.

A memory of you, collapsed on the couch –
the chesterfield you always called it,
"I need to lie down for a minute
on the chesterfield," which sounded
to me like a meadow, broad and tartan,
ready to embrace us; small and slack
you were, on the sofa, a hand across your eyes.

The husband and two eldest boys finally
out of the house, hustled through breakfast of
poached eggs and juice, bundled with brown bag
mock chicken white bread dutiful lunch off
into rain onto lumbering bus.

Eight a.m., drained and lost every day
on the field of sofa, too too surrounded
by the whiff of men like dark trees, long shadows
too much on the move, too much requiring.

Eight a.m., sprawled in the open, watched only
by a four year-old wanting someone to play with,
his need gone silent for a moment, then running
clear across your field of pain.

Our Lady of the Snows

Bonfires on the hills that ring
the city. Dark plumes rise
from cobbled alleys, the curbside
litter piled and set to burn.
Bona Night in Cork. Do the children
know why they light the fires?
They light the fires.

Down below, at the morgue end
of MacCurtain Street, the walkers
walk for Deirdre, behind the hearse
for Deirdre, removed at fifty-one.
Scores of mourners trail like shadows
behind their reasons. The city's
black-green river snakes nearby.

In Derrynane, the villagers
carry the dead across the strand
to Abbey Island's burial ground
by the sea. O'Connell's wife and
smuggler uncle are earthed there;
the King of the Beggars himself
lies in public elsewhere, alone
with his achievement.
We go for tea at the old estate
with one of his aging relatives
who calls out, "Betty, they're here,"
to his dead wife, as we approach.

In Montreal, at Le Cimetière
Notre Dame des Neiges,
metropolis of graves that layers
the west slope of Mount Royal,
the remains of my parents

fill two urns, their fires gone out
on this island of snows. Their ashes
shelved like jewels or old letters
in a bank box, niche #112M, walled in
with strangers on the crowded
flank of the dead volcano. Together
but nowhere near their own,
who fled here from various hungers –
Ireland, England, Wales; always
plenty of poverty to go around.

I wish for them a procession
like that of poor Deirdre I never
knew, or those villagers carried
slow across the sand as fine as snow
at Derrynane, buried almost as far
west as you can go there before
sailing off to the raw New World.

There was a kind of procession,
though. First the funeral, then
days later I sat with mother's ashes
on my lap as my brother's long white
car curled up past the lower graves
to the mausoleum. How strange
to carry one's mother so. I suppose
I sat on her lap enough to gladly
return the favour. She liked
to joke about her missing parts,
the surgeries she suffered. She might
have cracked a good one over this
final journey of her incinerated self.

Not much by way of tradition, just
this shadowy memory of her laugh.
It'll have to do. We deposit her
in the hillside vault, say some words
I can't recall, and leave the place like smoke.

Edges

the shoreline moves
with every lick
of lake
on sand

so do you touch me
and the space
between us
shivers

falls away
like a famous
mime's
parting bow

The Thin Uncertain Sky

Summer catches us unawares,
hurls us like new leaves
against its breezes.
It should be easy
to ride this sea of brightness.

Instead we fight it.
We walk through this city park
like rails of a track we balanced on
as kids,
clean parallels of steel
cutting a silent edge
into a narrowed distance.

This morning your love
was a silken trailing scarf
passed from one throat
softly to another.

I'm wearing it now
like salve against the gritty
wall of sun mid-afternoon
is building up against us.

Relentless summer changes
everything.
It's hard to know exactly why
we drift away – the blinded
flailing sun,
the yellow rage we don't dare look at
but feel between us
like burning rope
or the double curl
of a severed worm.

*

I hate obscurity,
    yet here it is like some fat
distant uncle suddenly in town
    to stir up trouble
among the relatives and strip
them down to their trembling
        truest selves.

This time I refuse
    to retreat into abstraction
where everything pretends
to make good sense.
I wish that everything
    were clear as eyes,
yours, wise as pre-dawn rain.

Another half-truth,
    for what about
  the way they spark like exploding
galaxies, or brim, or
haze over in the quickest
        shifts of weather?
Beauty to stun me every time
    like the moods
of mountain lakes.

In poems I used to call you
  ocean   elm tree   river,
swear you come from earth core,
  swing like a young
gymnast up and out
    to line of sure horizon,
disappear there into...you'd stop
  me to say

wait, I am a woman,
more like small imperfect
    wheel than river,
more searching and unfinished
   than the long thin-lipped horizon,
more frightened
      than the lithe-limbed acrobat.
I would say no,
you are a river.
I cannot afford your confusion,
the trouble in your eyes.

*

I have longed too long for clarity.
    Like images in a room
of magic mirrors
    it is everywhere and false.

What can I offer you now?
     If I were a child
beside a railroad track
    I could show you
      bits of coloured glass,
a piece of rope, veined stones,
handfuls of leaves,
        a twist of broken twig.

Now I don't know.
    I can only hold out to you
pebbles of a spirit
    continuously washing in
upon itself.
          No telling what either of us
will come to make of that –
   another kind of magic mirror
maybe.

*

In the distance mingling
winds and shadows move
across an uncut field.
We are walking, still, together.

I am coming to believe
in the thin uncertain sky.

A shell game I saw on TV
as a small boy...
riveted, in awe,
such slip and sleight of hand,
such wonders for the eye
it never mattered
where the pea showed up.

And one thing more – the subtle
shifting ocean of your feeling
toward, away from me, endlessly
alive.

The Middleman

Legs stretched out in a delicious sort of traction,
I lounge in the blue-green, low-slung beach chair

planted on the backyard lawn in the bright
slack middle of the last full day of summer.

Equinox. *Aequinoctium*. Half light, half dark,
the shift of seasons seeming suspended, neither

here nor there. And for reasons only half known
I hover between comfort and terror. Purple

petunias wave like dignitaries from the lavender
picnic table. The oddest thing – one minute

I feel tucked inside a dead-end safety zone, middle
of a middling life, pleasant home, decent

income, fenced backyard, a long good love.
The next I'm strung out on the thinnest

of taut high wires, the balancing act of a lifetime,
the crowd hushed below. Without ever

making a stir, I've stepped right off the platform –
a mid-life Flying Wallenda, cat-walking high

above ground. Look down beyond the tip of slipper
or think too hard of one side or the other

and I'm gone. Dead meat. Splayed on the seething
dump of career, TV, pumped-up media sex,

THE POETRY LIBRARY

the smother love of stuff... or else the cold bare
locker of denial. Never mind – even to think

of sad diversions slides a foot sideways
off the wire. Tonight a half moon will rise

over this wedge of middle America; I'll sip
a toast to that silky moon, especially the dark half

I can't see, shadowed by our world. But now,
in the lawn chair, on the equinox, working

the crowd of purple petunias, I'm right where I
have to be. Take another sip. Keep the balance,

kiss my wife, keep moving, bucko. I'm high
on my own thin wire, gamely stringing myself

along, half wanting to look down, half blinded
by midday glare, stretching for who knows where.

Mr. Anderson Is Alive and Must Get Used to It

1

A shimmery slant of golden light
is what you need tonight
to say you've made it through today.

Revise your life, front to back and back
again, as you go along. You'll like it better
the way it never was.

You're a cynical S.O.B., aren't you?
I don't think you know
your ass from your teakettle,
I don't think you know a hill of beans.

This coffee tastes better than it did
yesterday when I wasn't drinking it.
I am lost in thought. Ah, there you are.
How do you like it here?

2

Now I have forgotten
why I invited you all here.
You can go. You're no good

to me. I have nothing more
to say to you except maybe
that the evening light on the grey

garage roof just broke my heart
again with its dusty softness,
the subtle brush of remembrances
too small to be thought of

as history. I suppose
tomorrow too will be a splendid
day and we can mourn it
till it's done.

3

Mr. A, Mr. A, what is to be done
with you? You're leaking, Mr. A,
heart blood all over your suit. Kind

of shameful, really, except it's a little
like the truth oozing out. Show,
don't tell, that's what you used to say

to the students crinkling their smooth
smooth brows. They wanted all
the answers – tell me how, how, how;
shrewdly you repackaged questions,

shrink-wrapped, and never ventured
near the edges, or the core. Mr. A, what
do you say? Say more, Mr. A, say
nothing. God bless. Say less.

4

That clouded sky slashed with veiny blue
says all to me of spirit and of blood.
The life of the mind returns. Yesterday,

crowded with vacuums, laundry hampers,
the virtuous tools of prim enclosure,
I had succumbed, slunk, drooped,

become the tool of my tools,
a slug, a wrung-out thing, drear,
furrowed, sucked in, just some
dust in a bag, some trivial remains.

Today, possibility leaps, a bright fish
startled to find air and light so close
to this, its usual dark element. Blinded
almost, afternoon shyly knocking.

5

Too easy, too easy, Mr. A, you think you can
think it all away, this tightness in the chest.
On a winter day, snow flying and a worthwhile

job to distract you to distraction, you may
settle for world-weariness and the what
can you do, you've got to pay the bills

thousands would be glad to wear your shoes
what's wrong with you get on with things
before you lose what all you've got, it's a lot.
It's a duck-out, Mr. A, this settling, this crawl;

it's a pity, and so is climbing into thought.
The heart attack keeps ticking, Mr. A,
middle-aged blood backing up in the arteries
till it blows. Still time to change your clothes.

6

Duck-out, you say. Dachau. The tyranny
of purpose. Find meaning in each day?
Your problem, buster, not mine. The canary's
hanging upside down in the coal shaft.

I'm outa there. I'm anywhere. A job's
a job, and I'd rather be Batman, but I'll
settle, you hear, I'll settle for tedium
washed down with a pint of bitter. A song

is in order. I'm a Yankee Doodle Dachau,
Yankee Doodle do or die. In the toddler
years of the 21st century we ride our own

death trains festooned with flags and other
colourful stuff. At every stop we tell ourselves
but cannot hear, enough, enough.

7

Mr. A finds himself lost in the middle
of the middle aisle at Wal-Mart. Followed
a long line of cars to get here, thinking he'd
got caught in a funeral. It's a Grand Opening.

A sallow, bejewelled woman with raccoon eyes
is waving a credit application and promising
low rates. Life is great, he thinks. Smack
dab in the Cathedral of Acquiring, someone

wants to sell me money. What could be
more pure? Never mind the countless, beckoning
bins of stuff; buy the stuff you buy stuff with.

Plato would be proud, he thinks. Soon the idea
of stuff will be enough. And one thing more.
It could be worse. She could be my spouse, or yours.

8

Mr. A, you bring me down, you
really do. You dump on the here
today that runs between wrong and true.

You take the cool, easy line, Mr. A.
Does it mean anything to you?
I'm just a working stiff, Mr. A,

trying to get through. I probably
pay for you. Love me extravagantly
if you dare, Mr. A, it's the very least
you can do. I'm walking the wire

every day, Mr. A, I'm balancing
on the beam. I go to the meetings, I
move things along, I'm not
what you think I seem.

9

What's the use? I do not mean what I seem
to mean. A fork in the road means
choose, means use all caution, or lose some

options. Mind games on the left; to the right,
the cult of usefulness, the gore-tex and ziploc crew,
the woodstovers 'n hard drivers, the no-problem

bunch. In the middle, well, the middle's something
else. Good thing it's night, I can crouch and wait, rock
back on my heels, hum. I need me a feeling, you might say,
a passion. Get carried away, lose all time, forget the niggling

self, become the sudden blush on her neck, the dark-haired
beauty's laugh – all instinct and fraught with moment,
or memory. No use kneeling. Father Time is grim-lipped,
his eye on the hour; he's stuck with his tight little power.

10

Streetwalker back and forth by the curb, trying
to catch his eye. Steadies his gait, does Mr. A,
moves on; no one could say he rushed by.

Wellesley and Bleecker, a grey Sunday morning,
the fishnet stockings have had quite a night.
The legs below black leather skirt – long, slender,

verging on thin. Whipping him, taking him in.
But the hands are large, the shoulders broad,
the make-up on jaw, jut of hip not quite right.
In the eye, when he looks, sarcasm, a dare, a sailor-

to-sailor "What say, sailor?" grin. What shakes Mr. A
is he has no idea; he's flailing, he's swamped, overcome;
he's drowning in all he once was, all that he thinks
might have been. He shudders and hurries on in.

11

Mr. A, the grass. Have you noticed?
And the blooming bushes? Is that
forsythia? Tender and lush as babies.

Crab-apple trees like enormous
bouquets, wedding petals strewn
everywhere, tingeing with rose the day.

What will you do now, Mr. A?
Nothing. I can't seem to do
anything. Except pine for some
long lost chance I can't remember.

December is the blue in my veins.
But now it's May. Think arteries, Mr. A,
crimson as peonies, the silt-rich mountain
streams gushing red with purpose, or even,

to suit your midnight mood, the long silent
rivers of taillights winding home in an evening rain.

Postcard from Toronto

At the U.S./Cdn. border
an Ontario gov't billboard
promises, "We'll make you
feel incredible!" Five days
later, by God, I do.

On Toronto Island, having
ferried across a ribbon of lake
from the heat-hold of everyday
concrete and steel, we
are riding our little bike
ride among trees & cottages
of islanders who strangely stay
indoors, & we deserve this
little beauty, don't we?

While Quebec grows wan
in its long separation, the U.S.
heaves under the monied &
self-righteous flashing their
Contract along class lines
to slash at the lives of the poor
and the ill, & on the Akwesasne
Reservation we passed through
coming here, native Americans
straddle the New World border
selling millions of Marlboros
to white men on both
sides of the line. Nobody
seems happy about any of it,
not to mention the fireball
of ideology or is it meanness
incinerating the maps, the people
of Bosnia, Chechnya, etcetera.

Is this mail   getting through?
Forgive me   my bombast.
Weather is here.   Wish
you were lovely.
                              This border stuff
is dangerous   and everywhere.
Maybe I'll   go get a flag
of some kind   to stick on
my bike, or   wave
over somebody's   grave.
                              Listen closely
for the drums.   They echo
from isle   to isle.

Notice

the earring, its
flash and triangle,
the sheen of the chestnut
hair of the woman
alone at the table
across from the bar;
the curve
of the back
of the empty chair
facing her.

Rings

Life is not perfect like a gold ring, she says.
Something is off, she says.
It's not just do things all day, go home, kissy-poo
at night and that's it, she says.
Yearning, she says.
I have to go buy toothpaste, she says.
Call me, I say.
She says, Call *me*.

For Sharon

A woman walks
    through a swing door
& instead of a sunlit room,
    a pit, black marble walls
drop away beneath her.

A woman walks
    through a swing door
& instead of a sunlit room
    a field of purple loosestrife
rolls away before her.

A woman walks
    through a swing door
& instead of a sunlit room,
    an ivory pen, a notebook,
a name etched into the cover.

A woman sits
    down with pen & book
& instead of writing, begins to reflect
    on loosestrife & marble, the catch
in the breath when doors swing out.

A woman breathes
    from deep in her chest
& begins to sing a long slow song
    of flowers & pain, the openings
made by the high notes of need.

A woman begins
    to live the full shape of day
to day, waking the song that opens
    a door to the doors,
the ivory, the pages that wait.

Concave Love

Curled round you, resting – we're fronds,
a pair of spoons – I notice only the everywhere
you touch me, buttocks to belly, outside to inside
of arms and thighs, so near, my mouth your nape.
Drowsy warm in the ebb tide of a shudder, I have lost

my form entirely, mold myself to yours, take on
the shape you take. The ticking of the clock is just
another sensation, a drip that merges cleanly
with the woods scent of your hair. I recall
the photo you showed me earlier – Louise Bourgeois,

her sculpture of the arched, androgynous supine
form. *Arch of Hysteria* it's called, the figure so alone,
supremely convex, yearning. And Louise herself,
standing behind the piece, grinning and assured,
the mischievous maker leaning on her mystery.

What are we to her? A kind of kinetic art, maybe,
tendrilled, a four-limbed hetero shape bizarrely
tender in a gender-flayed time; the antidote,
the counterpoint, the untried edge of the sex game's
flipped-out coin. Let it be. We have a moment's grace.

Almost all that matters. We take it, we doze,
we barely listen to our deep, commingled breathing,
the complicated past, the fragile future drawn out
in every long soft intake, longer softer letting go.

Strait of Juan de Fuca

Crow flaps onto ship's railing
in the rain, in the sun, rain,
sun that happen here so oddly
often together, mixing and shifting
like a nervous teenager, foot to foot.
We pause in the unstated argument
brewing for days between us, neither
sure what it is nor if it's worth pouring
out – stale now, untried, bruising the air.

Then a rainbow, buckets of colour spilling
out either end into the sea, swathing
the big old bird on the bow, halo
over the whole shebang like a New Age
decal except for the low wet sky,
raw sea wind, tight-tucked wings.

Crossing from Victoria to Port Angeles,
the ferry saws the waves between
our countries. The border quavers
somewhere beneath the hard gray/grey
hull. We have time to kill and wonder
where is the line, anyhow, what does
it mean in this frayed middle scape?

Crow struts edgy, defiant along the stagey
rail. Big black caws roll back to us
like echoes. You laugh your great free laugh.
Yankee doodledo, I raise my hat to you
and toss it, oh Cana-dada, a wreath, a rainbow,
a preserver, way overboard. Crow twitches
those ragged old wings, then leaps off the ship
right through the spectrum. Quel spectacle!
We start to clap and nearly miss the loudspeaker
crackle, ladies and gentlemen, we've crossed the line.

Amendment

Huge orange sun tangled up in trees.
        We're getting to the end then.
Way back at the beginning there
    may have been a huge orange sun
carved by a rooftop. Hard to say.
        In between, pajamas, coffee,
an early visitor, a beer, anguished
conversation about the worth of something.
    Poetry anthologies. A poem by Berrigan
read exquisitely. A great deal more
anguish. The politics of saying.
A desolating trip to the laundromat.
Refusal to wash the car. A seat
    in the sun, with pigeons.
A seltzer in the cafe with friends. Some
hilarity about people born holding tiny
skateboards. Amazing numbers of people
walking giant dogs. A good-humoured woman
    locked out and making locked-out theatre
at the apartment window above the cafe.
        Calm laps swum while thinking
of, what else, an orange fireball involved
with branches. And a strikingly pale
    woman in elegant black slacks,
shirt, jacket, holding, in one hand, a string
        to a black balloon, and in the other,
the hand of a bobbing, blonde and bright-coloured
little girl. Some Sunday

And

is the key word here
    and is a quick link
and is a sprinting word
and you are 28 and suddenly
your life has bounds and you are
    stationary in its middle and
you can't quite believe that
        here is this and
    you are what are now is
and now you're 29 and older
than you will seem next year when
    motion starts again and
the existentialists were only kidding
you come to understand through repeated
    orgasm that Camus was only kidding
to the very end and
beginnings and endings begin to be
    important but impossible and
your life seems like a circle
like a sphere like a conical shrine and
yourself a dot inside it but nowhere
you can put your finger on because
your life is also inside you and
      you feel it in the morning fingering you
and now you're 34 and a little bit
broken and

At Button Bay

1

Nuances between us swoop –
a clutch of serious birds
just always out of reach

2

Among tall grasses you are
gathering loosestrife – long
stems of purple that pull
from you an amused,
a tender smile, as if sharing
a small foible or private joke.

Behind the lens eight feet away
mindful of heat and a wave
of impossibly wild beauty
I hold my breath
as I squeeze
down on
the suddenly
ruthless
shutter.

3

We meet late at night
trailing the day's events,
cover ourselves with layers
for warmth, cuddle
two separate darknesses.

The cat sleeps between us,
sprawled against legs.
Light finds the crack between
window blind and sill.

4

A year passes with certainty
diminished just that much;
you point out forsythia
proclaiming yellow by the road;
bold enough for faith, delicate
enough for truth; who
am I to contradict
such rooted, surging colour?

5

Sing our song and one day
die. Disappear. What we have
to do. The high blue note
left hanging. The leap of upstream
fishes in the sun. Sweet blinding.

6

Carnival of petunias
lovingly potted, carelessly
knocked over, remorse-
fully put back together.

Let me touch again
the small of your back
in sleep.

The Story

The cat curled
asleep beside
us on the sofa
holds his
little life
well, secure
for now
in his orbit
of pumped blood.

When one day
our slight
separate
tales of turning
stop, when
the blood
settles heavy
as mercury
in its dark
tunnels,
a river
impossibly
halted,
a long
blackened
mirror,
who will say
what has
occurred,
if we
carried it
off, away,
or what
any of it
meant?